Collected

MARIUS KOCIEJOWSKI, born 1949, is
He lives in London where he works
is currently completing a new travel book, *The Serpent Coiled in Naples*.

Also by Marius Kociejowski

POETRY

Coast

Doctor Honoris Causa

Music's Bride

So Dance the Lords of Language: poems 1975–2001

ALSO

The Street Philosopher and the Holy Fool: A Syrian Journey

The Pigeon Wars of Damascus

The Pebble Chance

God's Zoo: Exiles, Artists, Londoners

Zoroaster's Children and other travels

ANTHOLOGY

Syria through Writers' Eyes

MARIUS KOCIEJOWSKI

Collected Poems

First published in England in 2019 by
Carcanet Press Limited
Alliance House, 30 Cross Street,
Manchester, M2 7AQ
www.carcanet.co.uk

A CIP catalogue record for this book is
available from the British Library,
ISBN 978 1 784106997

The publisher acknowledges financial assistance
from Arts Council England

Typeset in Great Britain by XL Publishing Services, Exmouth
Printed and bound in Great Britain by SRP Ltd, Exeter

for Bobbie

Contents

Coast

The Water Clock

for J.

I will construct for you
Out of the words I think
Will work best this clock

Whose running depends upon
A steady flow we shall call
The imagination at work.

You need not be alarmed.
You will not be consumed
In a whirlpool of speech.

This clock is scheduled
By the simplest means,
A hole sized just so,

No bigger no smaller
Than that which the ink
Of this pen runs through.

Only what truly matters
Will be given clearance,
And this you may compose

Into whatever shapes
Will bring you nearer
To what you wish reached.

Do not think this comes
Without you pledging faith.
You must be prepared.

A level must be reached
Before the fulcrum slips,
And the hour is chimed

In so clear a pitch
You will think such sounds
Are made in heaven.

There is no beguiling
This level, not even
With mimicry of form.

You may pretend noon
But a shadow spreads
From where you stand.

And besides, be warned,
The horsemen will know
And will stay unmoved.

Night Patrol

What is there on a deep night in August
That conspires to lay a simple trap
Of moonlight, an empty road, a forest?
Why must a soldier guard his moving thought
Against conceit or against emptying
Into the imagined a last bullet?

The heavy insects knock against the wood
Of his gun as though in the instrument
Of death there is always a hidden light.
Behind a thicket the nocturnal beast
Drinks from its own shadowy reflection,
Its nostrils quivering at the coolness.

At each step he takes the soldier creates
A pocket of sound, a barren crater
Into which dust, pebble and stone spill back
As if to say, *Who makes the silences?*
Who is architect to these silences,
To all silence, if not a silent god?

The beast lifts its shadow from the water.
Listens. A ripple spreads along its flank
And through the fabric of all that listens.
The smooth leaf parts company with the branch,
And the owl blinks. The bearer of the gun
Absorbs through his body a disturbed earth.

The Return

Shopkeepers and jewellers
Stand in the doorways,
Their eyes full of whispers,
Their hands full of light.

I sustain such weight
Earth will not sustain.
The ground falls away
At each step I take,

As though to begin with
My feet had sight,
My feet were winged
But are now made blind.

Women in bright colours
Carry baskets of fruit.
I smell their ripeness,
The mingling of odours.

A bracelet slips down
The length of a raised arm.
I surrender to a city
Buried beneath a city

Where the morning bathes
The room in clean light –
The immaculate chisel,
The clairvoyant brush.

Woman Running

Where is the woman running to,
And who do you suppose she thinks pursues her?
The branches of the trees scratch her pretty face
And she can barely see as she stumbles
Over, across the broken world.

She has by mistake slipped into time
Where she is made love to without love.
A chill wind shrinks her heart to a pebble's size.
She is told that she must be always brave,
Always a companion to stone.

Dead Lovers

… Maestro, chi son quelle
Genti, che l'aura nera si gastiga?

The stones hold the ringing
     Of our steps clipped with steel
And the leaves our whispers:
     They seek our blossoming.

But earth turns with coldness
     Against husbanding sun.
Snow caps the bitter fruit
     We grow to nothingness.

Caligula's Death

They who need a clock
To tell seasons apart,
Who cannot plant a seed
And withhold all passion,

Who gather at noon
To slaughter a word,
Who wear a stiff collar
While poisoning a river –

Through them I journey
As I would a valley.
I have no argument.
I bear no enmity.

I slay only the loved.
Their tears are my own,
And their blood remains
On my hands forever.

Coast

1

We moved among delicate instruments,
Taking for a theme the sovereign light,
The scrimshaw, the parliament of water.
We then sought a division between things.

Once divided, truth divides forever.

We abandoned the angelic forms, smashed
Against the wood our heavenly quadrant,
Struck aimlessly from island to island.

2

We embraced without shame what was simple.
We wept to see the wild geese heading home,
The small blue flowers we could never name,
The women so ripe in their summer clothes.

The compass we held true is stopped inside.

We worship as pure the broken circle.
A blind foghorn sounds our way toward shore,
The old bleached houses dispossessed of love.

3

A band marching in circles slays a tune.
A megaphone blares garlands of welcome.
What should we return to, and what survives
Of love? And who are the boys skipping stones?

The shallow waters keep our image moored.

We were proud scavengers once, and we come
As ghosts here, savages brandishing grace,
With nothing to give but this our silence.

4

Speak kindly of those we have abandoned,
The innocent who in their madness strayed,
Who mistook for seraphim a bright lamp
Beneath the waters camouflaging death.

Such tenderness the depths would not abide.

There was nothing could be done to save them.
We trembled as the gulls swallowed their cries,
And as the distance took what else remained.

5

Who shall carry them across the harbour,
These stranger particles that seek congress?
We say words alone keep our nature whole
Against the hard weathering of fractions.

So what now siphons our breath from inside?

There is no way home, and the petty schemes
Are brushed aside, and the horoscopes too,
The mock images, the lights on the shore.

6

As with fish entering the broken hulls
Or the blind eel tunnelling through the weed,
So shall we make darkness our corridor.
We will by dead reckoning tempt fortune.

Go, catch the slightest air should any come.

It is better so than light which is false,
Better the rougher shape, the ruined voice.
Ask nothing more, as more would madden us.

Heat and Light

1

Things appear, glow, suddenly vanish.

A tree, for instance, can be so intense
It appears surrounded with dark light,
And just as the mind is trained to it
The prospect of certainty is yanked away,

A cut sapling gripped in the hand
And swung through air.

2

The distant explosions of a star –
The boy and his magnifying glass
Could set this whole scene ablaze.

The trees drop their leaves prematurely.

The path each leaf follows in motionless air
Is skilled by shape and weight,
In this stillness is itself wind.

A bucket is slung over a fence-post,
Its bottom a lacework of thinning rust.

3

The proximity of each object,
How each outshadows or is outshadowed
By its neighbour or else stands alone
        in exacting light –

There is no chronology.

The luminous signals are spread
Flat against the surface of memory,
As stars are discerned
Only by their brightness.

4

In the cracked geometry of the field,
A grasshopper climbs a dead stalk.

5

An empty bucket set
To rust on a fence-post –
That which extended the meaning of a river
Is a dead tunnel,

Holds nothing
But the bitter heat of intention
Soured by neglect.

The clanging emblems burn in mid air.

Shrubland

Say word finally came,
Would the withered plant
Have blossomed once more?
     Promise, primrose –
The petals fall from my mouth.

The ground is scattered
With fragments of objects
I can no longer fathom
     the meaning of.
They belong to an old
     civilization

Of whose inhabitants
I am barely able to speak,
Except that where they walked
     the birds exploded
Out of blades of still grass.

A hieroglyph of broken twigs,
The skeletons of small animals,
The sticking burr of thistle –
     Beyond remembrance,
There is only dull shrubland.

Babel

So it has come again –
Only the particulars differ.

There is such commotion.
Stones are gathered
Against a wooden door.

The voices are loud, indistinct.

I imagine torchlight,
A man pushing a wheelbarrow.
One could list endlessly,
Only where would that lead?

This tower they have conjured –
An architecture for the times,
Columns of stagnant air,
Emptiness upon emptiness.

The Stag

for Zbigniew Herbert

I

The predator blends with the innocent
And things of beauty make their betrayals.
The woodcock is sprung from its sleeping nest,
And once again we keep a chilled silence

As though wasps have settled upon our lips.
Our temper has been trained to this moment
As keenly as sight to the quick target.

2

The forest is a cathedral of light.
The sun swings a bayonet through the leaves,
And descends in slow widening columns.

A stag turns towards us, and lingers there
As though immaculately groomed for death.
He sees through the dark tangle of tendril
And branch the cold eye, the colder knowledge
We are what has always been said would come.

3

We were nothing in ourselves, nothing more.
If you must blame, blame those who merely watched
And who were brothers to none but themselves.
Were they not summoned as we were summoned?

How to say that once again darkness falls,
That plainness of speech ripens into song,
A nightjar swooping through its silences.
We are smuggled home to our sleek places,
The malevolent wasp its empty comb.

The Polar Bear

for A.

The polar bear in the zoo
Probes the night with his wet snout
And swings his enormous head.

The act is repeated and repeated,
A woolly thing wound up
And played to the finish.

It is the spring's madness:
How it imbues the wind
That blows across this city

Loosening shingle and bending branch
To where above your sleeping head
The window shakes in its embrasure.

I listen to your small breathing.
My daughter, I seek a connection
Between all this: these are distances

The stammering mind cannot hold.
A spider draws a line of thin silk
Across the room's impossible length.

If the thought seems hard
I could hum you a song.
But the immeasurable racks us,

So finally it is fathomed
Only by love and even then
Not so easily gauged.

The polar bear plods
Along the continual path
That runs through your sleep

And through me, and outside
The wind knocks still louder.
The spider curls into a ball.

You are nudged awake.
Sleep, child; it is only
A dream I made for you.

Doctor Honoris Causa

Doctor Honoris Causa

I should have seen the beard in the cradle.
And had my shepherd's breath raked your smooth face
I might have caught beyond those warbled sounds you made
The terrible, exact sentences they would become.
Should I have pressed the pillow to your voice?

                 I was your teacher once.
I taught you to see in the dark of ignorance
The shapes which certain words make and those words too
With which men who have something to hide sheathe meaning
      with mire.
I could not abide the way you handled a blade,
Yet glad I was when you moved with guile against your foes.
Who would not be proud to serve a boy who could bend with ease
      the bow of language?
We knew beauty once and we huddled close
Against the damp aching through our bones.
You learned to look deeply into the landscape
So that any sudden movement there would make your soul vibrate.
It is said you credit me with all this and more.

On a day more January than June, coldness where warmth should be,
I pull the blind on the swaying crowd outside.
The wind blows your speech about like a newly wrapped bundle.
You strangle the populace with your love;
The orphans in the street follow you home.
You may be shocked I still breathe.
A strange kingdom it is, where only the dead win prizes.
You should have honoured me with silence.
I send you the address where I live:
A blackbird sings outside.

If civilization is to be, we must have slaves.
Another voice speaks through the cold Assyrian stone,
The same words you spoke in Rome, Moscow, Albuquerque.
It hardly matters from what place they come,
The consonants of power remain the same.

Suddenly we burst upon that scene,
A warm day beside the Euphrates, the mood festive
And perhaps a little too forced to be wholly true.
A procession of musicians strums guitars and lyres.
It could just as easily be the Thames or the Yangtze:
We squeeze narrowly between boredom and pleasure.
A young boy is perched astride a wooden cage,
A lion milling back and forth beneath him;
And death being close sends a message of ice through the boy's
        testicles.
A serious joy is to be had here.
We find the alabastrine marble somehow remote,
And this chariot bringing on this other bearded voice
Is of a world too soaked with blood to revere.
There is only this youth we know from elsewhere.
A pale boy in Albuquerque siphons the sun through a broken bottle.
A young peasant visits Moscow for the first time.
We find him again flapping card in Rome.

A signal is made, and the boy waiting for a king's eyes to meet his
        pulls the release;
A couple of horsemen, ancient picadors, spear the lion towards the
        chariot's blinding noise;
A wall of soldiers bearing high shields blocks all hope of escape.
An arrow flies and will always fly across the stone.
Another arrow pierces the lion's shoulder and another the lion's
        spine.
As though smelling the high grape the beast with stunned eyes
        delves space,

But the air is too solid to probe any more.
The man who commits into stone these final agonies makes sure
      they are
As finely carved as the ringlets in the beard of the king who burns
      alive
The children of his enemies.
The sculptor faithful to what he sees will always be at a distance
      from what he serves.
A hardened pity makes these walls breathe.
The boy watches the king pour a libation of wine over the lion's
      corpse.
A weeping boy smashes his balalaika against a tree.
A tourist in the Via Sacra finds his wallet gone.
A small pile of twigs and leaves begins to flame.

If civilization is to be, you shall know the humble.
Old Blake painted your relative crawling on his hands and knees.
Smoke hangs above the tumbled brick which housed your throne.

3

Where can I find you absolutely alone?
And by alone I mean disencumbered of that solitude which comes
      of being in charge.
Alone as wolves are alone, and only in those silences which are
      purely mine
Will we speak through the straight and narrow of love.
The hour is late, the spade's edge sparks upon stone.

I hear that you regularly poison your slaves.
You will accuse me of being overly figurative,
And already you think to cure me with a doctorate,
A pension scheme and a gold watch which is of no use when for me
Only the blackbird singing in the branches is time.
It's a universe all rusty fish-hooks and spiritual collapse;
We must play our games in the absence of rules.

The journey begun in disburdened light stops here
Amid a heap of broken glass, distorted facts, prescriptions of all
colours and sizes.
We shall wear paper crowns, if need be.
So what do you suppose had become of me while
You were busy shaking the virgins from their trees?
The smell of greatness must have been too much upon me,
For I was sent packing from village to village, shore to shore.
There was no place so remote I could not find your smiling features
plastered everywhere,
A peeling icon sunned to pale greens and blues.
A valley of ghosts became my abode;
And still I sang your praises, thinking you might summon me
From the vaults where even now my brothers and sisters hide.
Yes, I saw my own dying down there.

When finally I returned home nobody would speak my name.
My scribbled notes were used to keep the mice in their holes and
the wind from coming inside.
I spent evenings following the moon upon the face of a river
So old it could remember nothing, no, not even the kings whose
chronicles I pushed into rhyme.
Who should know such neglect and be?

4

If ever you should make the journey here,
I will show you those few things which I call mine.
You will remind me that I once told you nothing can ever be mine,
And I will thank you for so kindly restoring to me my own tongue.
We must allow ourselves these solemn courtesies
Since anything else that can be destroyed you already have.
Say then that I am a slave to these several pleasures which I find
        hardest to release.
I have nothing else which you can remove.

This astrolabe a blind merchant sold me.
The man who made this table could neither read nor write,
And yet he could converse in the hidden language of trees.
I could heap the world upon this table.
A philosopher who can barely hold his wine tells me my wooden
        chair may not be here.
A phantom supports me.
This bed is sunken only to my own shape.
I could never speak of love although I mocked in verse its parlance
        once or twice.

I must tell you that I loved what was not mine to love, the mother
        of a certain pupil of mine.
A wild hyena stoked her eyes.
These books are prisons waiting for you or anyone else to set the
        words inside them free.
I must ask that you handle my pen with care.
Will you sentence this pen which obeys no hand but mine?
This narrow room is borrowed out of time.
I shall, if you allow me, remain here.

Giacomo Leopardi in Naples

Giacomo Leopardi in Naples

Do you know that something very strange is happening to me?...
When I think of my impending destruction, I seem to see myself lying in a ditch,
with a crowd of ribald fools dancing on my belly.

– Leopardi to Paolina Ranieri, 1837

Shall we, my sweet tooth, consume another ice?
I signal Vito *il padrone* whose grave nod bespeaks the substance
Of any man who knows what his art is,
And the making of ices is surely one.
I must beware my friend Ranieri who would deny me this sad pleasure
Although my clock almost strikes twelve.
Antonio Ranieri, who, if I could believe in God, would drive Him
 from my table
And then sermonize on the evils of chocolate –
This man whom I love plugs my brain with his cackle:
'The mood on the Largo della Carità spells plague,
And still, my Giacomo, you cannot bear to leave Naples.
What will you not gamble for Vito's matchless ices?'

All Naples is one huge, sleepless pantomime
As was that other place the gods covered with ashes.
The mountain broods beneath its canopy of smoke
While these revellers with their booming voices and pointed shoes,
These plumed creatures whom progress loves,
Make corridors in air.
The pursuit of happiness brings them none.
They drape the skeleton of all things with their festering pride,
And fearing the tumble through endless space wage war upon silence.
Should they win, where then my verses?

The ancients scorned the man who sups alone,
And yet what deeper shame than to be seen from above slobbering
 over an ice?
Or to be judged by the stains on one's clothes?
I should banish all pleasure to the cubicle.
Who, if suddenly the world broke, would probe the rubble,

And finding here my skull with a spoon stuck inside,
Summon up the pale flesh which covered the bone?
Would they conclude this man of words loved so much the life he
      could not have
That he loved death even more?
They shall review my bones from all sides,
Saying the darkness which goes so deep can only be pure sunlight in
      reverse,
Or, as that bastard Florentine said of me,
'There is no God because I am a hunchback;
I am a hunchback because there is no God.'
Bah, I'd rather that Vito bury me.
The place is suddenly hopping alive,
As if from nowhere all these people pressing close, their breath stale
And their talk even worse.
I shall command my own table.

I was born in a sepulchre.
When I consider the years swaddled in that dark place,
A cold, high room where the aching for knowledge doubled me,
Small wonder the world's light blinded me.
And now I shall perish where the mountain hugging the shore
      makes a cradle.

I must praise the bread a certain woman bakes.
You will not find such bread anywhere outside Naples although
      Genoa comes close,
And this madonna of the loaves is Genovese.
The world becomes for me a narrow place,
A simple truth Ranieri might consider when he comes to write my
      notice,
Although I fear the enthusiasm which in him outweighs intelligence
One day may become menace.
Already I gauge my own death in his voice,
And when he asks what my needs are, I say only those which he
      would deny me.
A doctor stands always by his side.

'You must quit Naples,' they tell me, 'Go, before the cholera comes.'
I shall not forsake the bread this woman bakes.
The fewer my needs, the more precise they must be
Should they make the narrow world bearable.

Perhaps I should love Paolina more.
The sister of Antonio Ranieri reads me verses,
And although Ariosto, Tasso, Dante sound strange on a southern
      tongue
I would swap heaven for the bright lamp in her voice.
She is so completely without malice.
The other night she stumbled over some passage;
A deep blush spread through the awkward silence,
And it was as though she wished she could hide behind the language,
Thus spare me the illusion of love.

La donna che non si trova.
The women on the Largo della Carità glide,
And if they seem to me of a world other than the one which
      spurned me
The plain girl who reads me verses
Shall be my earthly guide.

Antonio
      Ranieri,
            Paolina…

I will write in my book of consolations the names
Of those whom destiny might otherwise blur on stone.
The critics and poetasters must fend for themselves.
They would burn up the whole language for a single shred of praise,
Yet I alone give them credence.
When finally the swine dance attendance on me
(And yes, that one in particular who mocked my shape)
Will they say this man of words sugared his lemonade so it became
      a thick syrup galvanizing the flies?
An age whose minds are clogged with obscenities will note
What Vito, a man of honour, commits to silence.

A peasant from the Abruzzi plays on his bagpipe.
Ah, that I should have wasted breath bullying language
When this man with his solemn music pulls darkness over the bay
    of Naples.
Although God hides and Signor Leopardi must die
A sudden gladness swamps me.

Scende la luna; e si scolora il mondo.

Almighty blindness conquers me,
Yet still I see my silver spoon rise
And then dip towards the round horizon of my table where God is
    a flickering candle.
Perhaps Vito, the purveyor of ices, can say more of what pleasure is
And what place it has on the curve of the infinite than any struggler
    with rhymes.
On this night, however, let it be said some deep chord ancient and
    spare,
As pure in sound as anything Pindar wrote,
Cut a swathe through the clattering age.

A painted wagon thunders over the cobblestones.
Already I can hear from another, darker vehicle the hooded voice
Crying, '*Chi ha morti, li cavi!*'
But what is death when Madama Girolama bakes
The bread that shall always carry the sound of her name?
Vito places the chairs on the tables;
Moonlight sweeps the floor bare.
This is a strange forest which I must now leave.
Say Giacomo Leopardi found peace at Naples.

Night Song of the Nomadic Shepherd in Asia

after Leopardi

What resembles the moon, if not this shepherd's life? this always on
    the move?
O silent moon, you rise, and over these desert steppes
Where since early dawn I have pushed my flock your journey
    continues.
Mountain, shrubland, pasture –
Will you never have done with these old scenes?
Can it be they still hold your gaze while for me all pales?
Perhaps you should tell me what purpose our lives serve,
And where my brief passage and your endless one lead?

You see this man running over sharp stones, through gorse –
The high sun scorching him,
The cold wind blasting him.
You see him stumble and then springing up move with ever greater
    speed,
The blood filling his shoes.
The years blitz his scalp white.
At last, all strength in him gone, he collapses.
As hope is to the shrivelling apple what he becomes shall be
A dead wasp the wind shakes.
You see, unblemished moon, what this pilgrim's life is.

Man is born of labour,
The pain and the suffering which are his first knowledge.
Always, death is the midwife.
The parents cushion him, of course.
What finer thing is there? So much love, guidance –
But if misfortune rules, why should we endure?
And why sustain that life which we must console?
But my words do not sound beyond their mortal frame,
And anyway, you, eternal moon, would care but little for their sense.

You who know solitude
And how deeply thought goes,
You above all should know what this our sorrow means.
As death squeezes us close, our colour fades;
And when earth forgets us so too shall those we loved.
You spy some tender heart –
You see for whom spring smiles and what summer makes ripe,
What purpose winter hides.
You who know why things are,
What the dawn's fruit is like and the evening's too,
Will you not prove this shepherd wise?

You hang mutely above this dim landscape
At whose distant edge the sky becomes a dome.
And standing here, I ponder the vast solitudes;
I question all that moves, and, yes, even the flesh that bears my name –
All things revolve, go back from whence they came.
Yet I divine no scheme.
All is badness to me.

My sheep graze in silence.
They know not what is gone or the blow which must come.
I envy them their calm repose.
I envy them still more their not knowing by name
The pale, sickly creature which shadows me.
My flock, what joy is there and what joy can there ever be?
Such heaviness fills me, but although I drowse I shall never know
peace.

If wings took me among the stars, swept me
Where the strong winds whistle through the mountain defile,
Would I be happier, you gentle flock?
O wandering moon, would I be happier?
But dwelling too much upon those fates not mine,
I drift still further from my theme:
As the day of birth comes, darkness fills the stable –
Darkness floods the cradle
Of all which must be born.

The Wolf Month

The month which we now call January they called 'Wolf monat,' to wit, 'Wolf moneth,' because people are wont always in that month to be in more danger to be devoured of Wolves than in any season else of the year; for that, through the extremity of cold and snow, these ravenous creatures could not find of other beasts sufficient to feed upon.
Verstegan, *A Restitution of Decayed Intelligence*, 1605

Wolf's Words

Offspring of a bad principle, a whore's lot,
The Antichrist, child-eater, birth of the cool –
Where shall I say this black inventory ends?

A man singing psalms, mouth jewelled with sores,
Says nothing but good will come of my demise.

Idwall's Tribute 962

Edgar commands a Welsh king to pay him yearly a tribute of three hundred wolves. Their carcasses are brought to Wolfpit in Cambridgeshire.

Out of skins stretched
Upon racks of bone, eyes
Stare glassily towards

A cold periapt of sun.

Beneath snow,
A struggle of flowers
Mingled with humus –
Spring will rekindle
Processes of root and rot.

Flies will buzz, bow-like,
Across the heated amplitude of noon.

At the periphery of hell
The stench will be strong,
Almost visible.

Gospeller

Shot into an untuned eye,
The ricochet of light
Upon snow; so God's
Word blasted sight.

Pestilence is sovereign.
Amid the sturdy oak
I feel death hanging close.
Already, faith dwindles.

Winter has emptied bins,
Broken the stout hearts
Of men; children feed
Upon shrivelled hope.

The solstice falls short
Upon my day's work.
My staff's shadow
Returns to its wood.

I see the light of Acehorn.
God is kind. I will soothe
My sorrows with hosannas,
My spirits with barleycorn.

The Woodcutter

A ringing of metal
Against frozen bark –

The muscles quicken
Along the arm, ensuring
Steady swing of chopper.

This man felling trees
Is the perfect master
Of his own solitude.

Unfriended, unblest –

With measured aim
This stubborn metronome
Slays time, embraces

The company of wolves.

Penitential

Acehorn, a hospice

I

Smoke spirals towards
A cold, thinning heaven;
And so the foolish minds
Of men shall be dowsed.

God is triumphant.
I whisk from the flames
Another glowing parable.
O, worthy scribe!

I am newly pricked,
Spurred by that thought
As oxen might gladly
Master a servant's switch.

2

My host brings food,
A pilgrim's allowance.
I perceive God's will
Upon slow, crippled feet.

I, for the present,
Must learn to accept
Such sibling kindness
With humility, bless

What comes. I am touched.
The mead is amber light
Spreading through my veins.
Ah, poverty is rich.

3

I am almost nothing
But touch, these fingers
The weights and measures
Which serve my reason.

The one thing holds me
Against flying apart is
This cross which hangs
Upon me. Proud amulet.

Sleepless, sleepless –
Will day's journey ungrip
Me? Whose eyes are these,
Swarming in the bushes?

Clearing

Evil is pushed back, muzzled behind stalks of Good grain, trees are felled.

The Wolf Month

A wolf first seeing a man begets
a dumbness in him.

Yes, it staggered him.
The tongue rolled back
Speechless; the body
Slackened upon its rack

Of faith. At his approach,
Dogs twisted at the ends
Of chains, teeth bared;
Cows dropped calves.

Women sheltering children
Under smudged aprons threw
A sweaty coin in his path,
Slung stones at his back.

A black drop entered,
Burst the thin veneer
Of piety. Yes, despair
Shook him as from above,

Swallowed him whole;
And now his staff prods
The stony ground, traces
Blindly the face of God.

Polson's Quarry 1743

The last English wolf, so it is said.

Blood flecked
Upon broad leaf –

Never has such greenness
Known such redness.

The forest is full of mirrors.
Death is relayed
From branch to root,
Rock to unblinking eye.

A farmer named Polson
Wipes the blade clean.

Wolf's Weeds

A shadow hidden deep within your own shadow,
The one you would rather not see still breathes,
Or should I say, is not quite extinguished.

A world almost gone, bah, the man in robes spumes.
Such fools they are, who destroy only themselves.

Tiger Music

Tiger Music

You see that eminence?
You shall have your heart's fill of them there.'
The village elder, almost blind, pointed to a crag floating in distant
    haze.
        Thus sped with hope,
Our guns cocked, although it never was our purpose to kill, we went
    looking for tigers.

If what the *fellâhîn* said was true,
If there was nothing they could not, in their language, describe,
We met not a soul who knew all the words, the more than fifty or so,
That speak the many shades of tigerness between one which dozes
And another that lunges,
        the different music they make.

All day we watched for movement in the stone.
We saw lizards which at our approach slid off like lightning into
    crevices.
A couple of eagles from an eyrie
                on the crag above
Wheeled and hovered, their shadows like two
Spots of ink moving upon the mountain-side.
We watched for tigers but saw none, although we did see
A gazelle, its gashed throat jewelled with flies.
Whiteness pooling his eyes, the village elder
        was confused or so he appeared.
'What could have made them go away?' he asked. 'Once, I saw
    tigers everywhere.'

All night we fought among ourselves.
One man said leopards dwelled here, while another lynxes.
Anything but tigers, such was the consensus of all but one.
The old boy stuck to his guns, of course, warned us
Of the dangers that come of grabbing tigers by the tail.

'A snake doubles back upon half its length,' he said, 'whereas a tiger
    goes it whole.'
Our dragoman, scoffing at him, said this was
A country as bare of tigers as his soul of truth.
'So why, then,' the other replied, 'if indeed there are none,
Should our language have fifty or more words for the many moods
    they strike?'
                          We drank our bitter coffee,
And discussing what provisions we should take,
Said tomorrow perhaps would see the settlement of our dispute,
As to what those famous tigers really were.

A Seventh Jew

E lucevan le stelle…

A darkness such as this he can almost taste.
                              What else?
Smell, oldest of memories, he smells her fragrance.
And what else? At the end of a garden path sounds of a creaking gate,
A patter of footsteps that makes heart leap like a hare,
Almost too fiercely for its slender cage.
                              Anything else?
Yes, he who has never loved life so much as he does now
Covers with kisses the nakedness of her face, sings as he would
        before a heavenly judge.

We owe him so much more than just our lives,
This Jew from Lyon who, if only he had trained his voice,
Might have made, if not the big rôles, then operetta perhaps.
Still, there's no saying what in odd circumstances a beginner will do,
As when he learns this may be his only chance
And the one whose part he sings is about to die.

                    We imagine just how it was,
Seven men pushed down the corridor's bright glare to the courtyard
        beyond,
As if allowing them to go in peace would destroy the bigger scheme
Which was to make men less than what they are.

                    The names of six survive.
Of the seventh, the anonymous one, we know only he was a Jew
        with a fine voice,
Who, from behind bars, made true a certain woman's perfume,
A meeting at dawn beside a garden gate.
What is any history of resistance, if not this voice tender
Yet strong enough to remove from other men's ears extraneous
        noises,

The squeaking of boots, a key scraping in the hole.
As he sang whose face did he smother with kisses?
So finely registered was this performance, so pure his timbre,
Somebody there simply had to take note.

Full Force

i.m. Christopher Whelen

1

We watch as they warmly embrace,
This couple we think of as foes.

We must let them pass unhindered.
We must keep from them our applause,
As they reckon what joggles the spirit is worth double
What smarts behind the eyes.

They walk along the downward path,
Speaking of all things small rather than large.
The pebbles are sometimes loosened,
And rush ahead like smooth heralds.

2

They breathe deeply the crop of late,
And there beneath the harvest moon push as one
Through the turnstile of speech.
We must spend shrewdly their silence.

The stars have come out in full force.

The old bruisers standing in the middle
Of the field study them until their necks begin to ache.
They grow heavy with fatigue, for
Although their hearts are open wide
Their minds are sealed against the infinite as against death.
They are at too tender an age.

We watch the slight, bent silhouettes,
Almost clownish, as they trudge home.

A Pavane for Sydney Housego

When Sydney fiddles, Bach fumes in his grave.
                                    Mojo whines.
Mojo, ears bigger than his master's, listens to the music of the spheres,
Which is why when Sydney scrapes at the violin he drops snout
        between paws,
And, from as close to the ground as possible, stares into his beloved
        tormentor's face.
A man plays badly yet to his own ears well enough to force the
        applause
Of the scowling angels he keeps on low salaries.

            Sunlight twinkles through the leaves.
What is there on a day such as this that allows for a massacre,
This old man on a park bench busking for pennies,
Against whom Johann Sebastian Bach could bring a charge of
        murder in the first degree,
Whose mangy dog presently yowls at the skies?
Sydney could play for a thousand years, never once improve.
            The angels in the branches wince.

A man hears the voice he would most like to have.
So rare, one who closes the distance between what is and would be.
All too common, one who thinks he has done so.
Sydney Housego is free of any such scruple, not for him splitting
        matchsticks with an axe.
The violin was not made for a sap wearing kid gloves.
A chunk of the savage goes into making a thing fine.

A small girl in a red dress trimmed with white lace
Watches from the sanctum her childhood is, where the light has no
        visible source.
If church for her is these arching trees, its priest this man at the fiddle,
The silver collection plate is a tin can once home to a dozen sardines.
She drops a coin there, quicksteps back to her parents who invited
        her to do

What they might like to have done themselves.

The only acknowledgment she gets is

A slight nod, as much as anybody loath to interrupt the flow of his
art is prepared to concede.

Suddenly,

Mojo spotting a squirrel chases it through the bushes.

All of civilisation will not bring him to heel now.

The violin stops.

The angels make a dash for the exit, big azure skies.

Sydney whistles, then shouts the only thing any one has heard him
say for an age,

'Mojo, Mojo', as if his mouth were full of marbles, or rather, empty
of teeth.

Alas, Mojo's gone.

Sydney puts his instrument even more out of tune than before.

The angels, bored, go back to their places in the trees.

The girl stares at the hole Mojo made in the bushes.

A harp dug up from the graves at Ur,

A sounding disc of stone from the Malayan jungle –

Should the instruments change, no matter, banjo & clavichord are
born of a single creature.

Always music comes from inside, which is how the gods give,

Which is how one who plays only because he has to receives.

Mojo returns, squirrelless,

So much tongue spilling out of his mouth, heavens, where does he
keep it all?

Saliva flecks Sydney's face.

If he fails to notice, not so the small girl who giggles.

The fact is, he plays just fine, better than any one has ever done
before.

The notes leap from the fiddle strings, grow invisible wings

That bear them beyond our stubborn knowledge.

The angels jabber among themselves.

We need him too, who figures this world his bench,

The smaller without whom the greater can never be.

We must now salute Sydney Housego, tap our bows,

As we make ready to perform for him this pavane.

Sonata & Prelude

Dinu Lipatti plays Chopin's Sonata in B Minor

What harmony is this?
The Tempest, III.iii.19

...an Hieroglyphicall and shadowed lesson of the
whole world, and [the] Creatures of God...
Sir Thomas Browne, *Religio Medici*

Says: God the plumber comes,
A pair of oily cloth gloves, asks her what the problem is.
Answers she, the ghosts banging in the pipes, saying come,
Our heaven's a Magyar village.

Ah yes, God replies, those Chinese again.

Are you there, hello?
The woman from Budapest fumbles for a cigarette,
A slow poison the quickest cure.
Likewise, she says, the men who spread ordure with their shoes,
As puzzled in their world as she is wise in hers,
Who go as they come, in a flowerless haze.
Sweeping up the traces, she knows better than to blame,
Says almost anything's easier than love.

She lights a thin green candle.
Appears not to notice,
Or perhaps she does, the top buttons of her blouse are undone.

A cormorant invades the bones of her face.
She pulls a record already an antique from the battered sleeve,
Which she holds by the edges with reverence.
Candlelight spills over its surface.

Says Dinu Lipatti as though the name
Were a prayer and not at all a name, she says he came as close
As anyone may come to music's absolute.
Listen,

As best you are able catch the small notes,
A sparrow's chatter behind a blackbird's tune,
A semiquaver in the voice, segregating false from true,
A mandolin shedding pale coins through the leaves.
So much escapes, spoils beyond our notice.
Listen, as to do so with a depth proper to the performance
Will be to compose within ourselves
An umbrella over all the newly bombed sites.
Would that he touched the random notes of my life,
Says she, her words bleeding into silence.
                                        Are you warm enough?
Should you not be, come, sit by the candle.
A prehistoric needle drops into the groove.
A hiss at the beginning of time, band one, is a length
Of silk pulled through a hand squeezed a little, the clicks embers in
        dying fire.

                    Winter comes, the radiator explodes.
A woman alone hears things her fancy translates into images,
She would rather not say what they are.
                                Says one must make
Of disparate elements (ah, why not desperate?) a habitable place.
You may pour another glass of wine.
Would you not say our wines are closer to the taste of blood than
        those of France?
                    Says while listening to music
We should not close our eyes, or else we remove a world not ours
        to remove.
                    If song is only sweet reverie
A fool's lulled not by love but love's perfumes.
And did not Shakespeare's couples listen with their eyes?
Where did Dante first hear light's absence?

                        Allegro maestoso,
We may briskly and with majesty progress to the next course,
Says she, pushing an apple across the table.
If you were to slip the years like a robe from these shoulders

You would find me approaching for the first time the conservatoire,
A girl inflamed by the sounds of the instruments coming from deep
     inside,
And for whom love was this, a ghostly tinkle.
What I learned was that every note in every phrase must live,
All parts give meaning to the whole.
A professor I had there, a man with a monkey's face,
Who, when I visited him to say my goodbyes,
Whispered, as though afraid his voice might carry to another
     province,
Asked me whether it was not true, that music is made solely in and
     through time.
I watched him peeling an apple, slowly turning the apple
Against a blade that he held perfectly still while the peel spiralled to
     the floor.
I found beauty in this, as though nowhere else.
                'Ah yes, Soul, of course!
Yet what's Soul,' he cried, 'without a metronome? without Time
     and its sister, Space?'
        'You must forgive me,' he said, 'if I tremble.'
And fool that I was, wrongly I heard a semiquaver in his voice;
I would have to flee this poor monkey with his apple.
          'Would you help me solve a riddle?'
And, with calmness approaching terror in his eyes, the old man spoke:
       'Our world bearing all the things we love
Will one day be swept like a burnt pea into space,
And the idea, the sheer audacity of it, makes me dumb with rage.
Such are my days, punishing apathy with scales,
As though a man clutching a baton might change the direction of
     the universe.
Would that it stopped there, but no, something else makes me stare
At the alarm clock's fluorescent face.
         Suppose Bach made a mistake,
Yes, the great Bach, in thinking his angelic voices
Would reach the ears of One in whom I believe and in whom I do
     not believe.'
The professor soon to be emeritus dabbed his eyes.

The apple's flesh began to turn pale brown where the afternoon sun
    fell at a plump angle.
                        'If indeed music's condition is time,
Young lady, by what powers in the cosmos can it be heard by
A God enthroned beyond time?'

                        Ah listen, she says, the cantabile!
An Italian scares the German out of the Pole, Bach and Mozart his
    sworn guides.
What you have is Bellini, opera! One could easily drown in waters
    such as these,
Yet this man who plays with reticence, sans caprice, makes
A wedding between freedom and discipline.
Would you mind if I smoke another cigarette?
Only as strong as she is fragile, she brings her face close to the flame,
The shadows flushed out of young wrinkles.

            Woman, who plays if not for your sake?

                    Says he was dying at the time,
So weak he had to be supported onto the stage, Dinu Lipatti
Who played as if the pale Chopin sat by his side,
Whispering, put the *rubato* here and not where others say it should be,
Yes, you shall be my sublunary advocate.

And so, cracking a joke between themselves, again they briefly live,
Whom the angels served but could not save.

            You ask whether this is not miracle?
What must the world be like, O, what must we be like,
If between all that is and our crying solitude
A man with the shoulders of a wrestler plays a note
At once firm and gentle, which hanging there is also its opposite,
A scudding moon dressed in silence?
What are we who seek for truth in tones?
A miracle to be true asks of us not that we fall to our knees,
Only that it be worthy of our justice.

Says she has never mastered the finale.
The woman from Budapest blows out the candle,
Says playing Chopin is for her like being made love to,
She who is no man's, only music's bride.

The Charterhouse at Valldemosa

His soul was flayed alive: a crushed rose petal,
the shadow of a fly made him bleed.

George Sand, *My Life*

I

Snow caps the pomegranate,
                            a buzzard drops through white
air, plucks a sparrow from the ledge.

                                   no again no
A man pulled alive from the dream's wreckage stares.
Quickly too quickly his coming-to,
                            a screeching through space.

                   Consider where he only just was,
a salon on the Rue de la Grange-Batelière,
                   the chandeliers like women's voices -

Suddenly, this monk's cell with its coffin shape,
                   an unfinished prelude spread over the table,
         a sprinkle of blood on crumpled lace.

                                   Savage isle.

     All's hell to one who seeks paradise.

2

The French lady with a manly name,
a musical Pole with an ashen face,
                    this couple of fools both wise
    watched the steamer's phosphorescent wake.

    A hand flung over the bed's edge
                        skims old waves.
            Was it a month or a century ago
a weekly packet from Barcelona puffed for paradise,
    the steersman chanting a tune?

A few drops of rain silently explode
                    against the windowpane.
    A piano floats by, out of tune.

            Majorca seeped through their eyes,
a bobbing row of windmills, skull-white,
            wooden sails beckoning them ashore.

The steersman spat into the waves,
                as though here's where one goes only
        for squealing trade.

A man bringeth culture, pigs what he takes.

3

Wind sobs in the ravine.
A bungling of hemispheres,
                              a cold winter in the soul
                where summer ought to be –

While others made ready to leave they came,
                              whom the world made gentle,
                mindless of the almanac's yellowing edges,

                a dead spider pressed between its pages.

A *signora* in trousers, an aura of cigar smoke,
                                                godless,
the consumptive, burrs stuck to his town clothes –
What need have they of guidance who can afford escape?
The ascent to Valldemosa was a Spanish farce,
                ¡ha! an upright pulled by mules.

Aurore, my white gloves?
                She and her children have already gone
                to the valley for milk and potatoes.

Shivering, he pulls from the table
                the pages of his unfinished prelude,
                its opening phrase, D flat major, sunshine.

4

Opening bars resonant of clear skies,
                        though to describe them so,
        and not as the azure we carry inside,

or, if pointing to where the mountain gouges
                        the cloud's belly,
        we ask what this man's playing has to do
                        with things as they are,

        what we do is reduce the sublime phrase
                        to a squeaking weathervane;
siphons we become,
        through which world passes merely.

As the broken arch suggests the whole,
                        so these fragments he composes
        are measures flung against the infinite.

                A blanket wrapped about his shoulders,
sweating, he aches to be where
        all things may be seen from all angles.

        A single chord perhaps will find him there.

        Says the C sharp major, not so.

5

So what of this woman with airs and graces,
                          whom Flaubert describes as
        'a man who calls herself George'?

                    She moves with deadly innocence,
a jug of milk slopping from side to side,
            a flowered bag cankered with potatoes.

                    Say love plays them in tones
ear does not pick up but Soul does; say love blinds her,
        Revolution's child, to his *ancien régime.*

She never was for ordinary life
                          who, when young, kissed her father's
        freshly-disinterred skull.

A few drops of rain fleck her dark and oval face.

                    Soon the road's barely passable.
Mud splatters her clothes
                          as she paddles up to
        the walls of Valldemosa hidden in haze,

    she who hears music in unearthly places.

6

Wet moonlight silvers the broken arches,
the monks' graves anonymous beneath the lemon trees.
        Darkly he plays the same note
                                over and over,
    watching through the music he makes
                        their drowned faces
            staring at his from the bottom of a lake,
a waking dream so terrible
                    its dreamer holds himself to blame.

        Suddenly, the dream plays them in reverse
so now it's he who watches
                    from beneath the water's surface,
        icy drops from heaven

    falling   over where his heart is.
            one by one

The door opens: she and her children shiver there,
                                their mouths blue,
    while he jumping to his feet cries,

            'Ah, I knew you were dead!'

7

A single thread of sound
                              stitches together hell and paradise,
        as precisely his now finished piece does.

She whose industry keeps them alive
                                          says, 'Listen,
        can you not hear the dripping on the files?'
                              A finger moves up and down
as if conducting from a score this one note.

                    She tells him he has composed this,
as he has already done
                              the famished cry of an eagle,
        a guitar playing a bolero in the distance,
                a sparrow piping beneath wet leaves.

                'What, imitative harmony?' he cries.

Anger winches him from the bottom of the lake.
                              'A child slavishly follows nature,
        whereas music plays inside me.'

        Only the furious dialogues hold true.

8

A cart thunders down the slope,
                    its passenger coughs blood and phlegm
          beneath an almond's flowering branches.

As with everything this white plague touches
                              the springless vehicle is
          afterwards fed to the flames.

Later, on his dying berth, he listens to
                              the squeals above.
All bound for pig heaven the vessel heaves,
                              the pink cargo slides.
          The stench is unbearable.

'Where's music in this?
                    Should we discover God here,
          if only by the shape His absence makes?

Aurore, will you find for me my white gloves?

                    She presses a damp cloth to his face,
she whose powers to cure
                    are beyond her knowledge.

9

Awakes, from what, into where,
                            fresh linen crisp against his face,
        a pillow scented with lavender.

A clock ticks in the pale corridor and, somewhere beyond,
                a jury of disinfected voices
    whose monotone spells assurance of a kind.
Although he's much too fastidious for existence
        earth must bear him a while longer.

                            What music is, his life is:
a prelude that supposes what it is prelude to exists already,
        if soundlessly so.

Slippered, he moves to the conservatory
                                where the Pleyel is,
        performs what he hardly believes his.

A buzzard swoops through this high room of pearly white;
            the tip of a spread wing brushes the chandelier.
    It tinkles.

                        She at her escritoire writes,
    the sound of her pen a sparrow pecking seeds at the
            window ledge,
'He no longer spits up blood, sleeps well, coughs little,
        and above all is in France.'

The Ghost of a Razor Blade

Communiqué for William Hoffer

Bill, wicked men gnaw at their own ankles.
Our troops bivouacked at the border of silence beam messages
Of massive defections from the other side.
The smirkers flee, throwing their ABC's to the flames.
Slow leaves tumble, a kazoo sounds the battle charge.
We put down steel traps, calling them prizes.
All this is bright lies, our army a phantom one.
An avocado is not a grenade, but we who make it so,
Who grow rare orchids or collect wooden toys, analogize
A sterile peace from which nothing of value comes.
Meanwhile, winter creeps into the greenhouse through its many
       smashed windows.
The absurd growths within freeze.

Smallholders, we plunge deeply our stakes,
And holding our small patches of ground we lose
The world to thoughtless jackasses, spineless,
Who'd have us believe miracles come by mind alone.
They speak from a chamber of dying echoes.

Who's this squeezing a Japanese rubber ball, his
Anger which in refusing to explain itself makes us wonder
What gastric condition leads to such grimaces?
Says he just happens to be passing through. So,
Why this battle with a street map twice his size while
Trying to hold an umbrella at the same time?
A sudden gust of wind blows parks and avenues, public
       monuments in his face.
Will anything ever, he cries, fold back to the old creases?
As of late he's taken to wearing loud colours,
Repeats words and phrases as if they're divinely shaped pebbles
To be held in the mouth while meditating.

We hear wisdom, or does the stomach rumble?
We sample his cheap fare, lovers who seem to stand for lovers,
Children who seem to stand for children.
And what's this spongy thing calling itself Love?
Such words when first heard cut through the ice within ourselves,
Only this time are spoken louder than ever before,
Capitalized, italicized ... signifying nothing.
When do we go back to hunting real beasts with real weapons?
Such bold language he uses, by which we mean verbs, nouns and
    adjectives,
Parts of speech never grown past kittenhood.
All believing themselves prettiest they disagree with each other.
An omelette of superlatives, they make
What this shark in maroon calls style.

The soul is not as fragile as it would like to be.
Bill, the fact you are a warrior and write only in aid of being one
Makes you invulnerable to almost anything they have.
Their old shield of protection becomes flimsy,
Weak enough to let deadly objects through.
(Will our springing you into the present tense,
As though you're still alive, make heart believe it is so?
What is our embalmer's art but making the dead seem about to
    breathe?)
A bookseller by trade, the instrument you were was delicate
Enough to pick up the faint traces of ozone
A rare book leaves in its wake, as when an electron passes through a
    cloud chamber.
So too, the words you wrote linger like perfume:
'When I attack I imagine the fire bird guides me to the exact centre
    of battle;
Of the thousands of arrows I fire
Not one fails to find its mark, but when there are no women, no
    books, no wars –
When the fire bird sleeps and there are no more enemies, I am
    unemployed utterly.'

Would you prefer we kept the news simple?
A windy night in November, which year it is matters little
Although oddly enough the hour does,
As when death came for you at precisely three in the morning.
There is a sound of crickets, although the season says no, no, no,
     impossible,
Must be the workings behind a tired man's eyes.
Questing moth looks for somewhere to settle.
Such music they make, these five lemons in a bowl of Prussian blue.
The furnace rumbles. Good night, forever.
A young widow in Moscow burns candles.
A soldier goes forth in the name of love.

Aurora Borealis

for George Johnston, on his 85th birthday

Who dares pick a bone with Aristotle?
The ghostly light he describes is like smoke,
A burning of straw in the countryside.

Wise Pliny made the world his catalogue,
Says when the Lacedæmonians lost Greece
An aurora mocked their galleys in flames.

The Vikings, of whom Johnston may be one,
Saw blond Valkyries swooping through battle,
Their brief to gather up the dying heroes.

What science says, a jongleur may endorse.
A solar wind brings Sun's charged particles;
They gather above earth's magnetic pole.

What happens then, the elements collide.
The electrons knocked sideways, as by love,
Warm the ions to a tremulous state.

Three pounds of starstuff childishly simple
When compared to a flickering in the nerves
Which may, with luck, translate into image.

This elderly gentleman with young eyes,
A gold wire spiralling through his earlobe,
A Viking in pale mac, speaks his verses:

Whose hat is moving on the water's face?
Alas, *poor Edward's* (stanza one, line three):
We must pray *for Edward and his trouble.*

We never get to make his acquaintance,
Yet what one watchful in his craft does is
Construct, with as few words as possible,

A sly dirge for the man of misfortune,
An asylum where he may dry his clothes.
We pity him who perhaps never was.

A dab hand, he makes his art look simple,
Although Valhalla knows the wild tumble
With the Muse, a soul covered with bruises.

While sadly he maps poor Edward's absence
The northern lights sway above our heads like
A woman sashaying down heaven's catwalk.

Whether they really do move as a whole,
Or rather, their atoms, gathering strength here
And dimming there, play upon our senses,

As they do, so dance the lords of language.

Salvatore Giuliano

Quid facies odio, sic ubi amore noces?
What will you do in your hatred, when you are
so cruel in your love?

Ovid, *Heroides*

I

We can almost smell the spent cartridges.
These gaunt figures with their wide moustaches are ambassadors
    come,
As from beyond the grave, counselling reticence,
Saying, *Speak only those words which do not hide what things are,*
And keep thought constantly on the move.
Who are these guns for hire, mouthing parables?
We ask them whom they serve, and, rubbing their stubble,
They hiss, *The ghost of a razor blade.*

The hills deepen with mauve,
And the bloated sun slides, bleeds over the distant pines.
The hour is all nerve.
As though piloted by some ghostly flame,
Suddenly we flare with one whom the devil in ourselves
Gave rise to, a tough who shook this isle.
What does death do with such handsome features?
A phantom of the kind engendered by dialogue
Slips between the colour of what is and the colour of what was,
As smoothly as a hawk on the thermal.

We debate how certain matters came to be,
And so, with a solemn measure that redeems time, we put bare wires
    to
A myth dipped in formaldehyde.

All geared up to mock sleeping justice,
Our brigands prowl through the village.
They observe, while pretending not to, every move we make,

While somewhere, deep within ourselves,
We can hear their dark, tracking voices:
Psst, the gun slackly held shoots wide.

2

You wished always to be of the people,
And even though you brought them trouble
Who among them would not provide solace?
And who among them would not break the law to preserve the code?
O Turiddu, very flesh of their silence,
You began as some Galahad on a shiny bicycle, upholding justice.
What loser did not bask in your presence?
So who was that other who came, blasting a hole through the haze?
Who gave shape to the darkness behind the hedge?
You were barely out of the cradle, malevolence came,
And men in their dismals began to slide.
A farmer whom misfortune drove over the edge sharpened his knife,
Watched the sun flash upon it, then heard the metal talk,
As talk it must have, for you saw the man smile
While he cupped his ear to the speaking blade.
A butchered snake dangled from the sacred olive tree;
Smelling the strange blood of that creature,
You thrilled to the knowledge of what makes things cease to be.
Pain and death absented themselves,
As though the pity of those words would make you hesitate.
Speed was to become a kind of virtue.
Your whole body drained with the pleasure the mule kick
Of the gun as you watched the sparrow plunge,
Although what you saw was only the slow image of something just
        gone,
An apostrophe hanging in space.
A scream flew up out of the bramble.
What it really was came from deep inside your throat,
A cry so primitive you blushed for shame.
Here, where the blood of many flows as one,

You would listen to the singing in the nerves,
And, spotting at once a false note, you'd strike as the adder strikes,
Without sorrow, without malice.
This, you darkly swore, the moment requires,
As to parley for but a second more would have been to see the
        hawk as dove.
The results you dumped in moonlit squares,
A note attached to each bundle, saying this one spoke, or that one
        took a bribe.
Weep, mothers and daughters and wives.
When finally the moment towered above all else, all time stood false.
The love you fought for, you wrapped in ice.
Your vanity was the vanity of the people,
And the photographer your only muse.

3

All day we grapple with slow commerce,
And now, with tiredness hanging upon us like shackles,
We face the dangers of the interlude.
There's everywhere the stench of failure.
Pah, spit our mild killers, cocked with pride,
Why not complain about the price of oranges?
Signori, you have not come all this distance just to lose
What by the stars above is your mandate.
You might better petition the moon than seek to communicate with one who
        rumbles in the grave.
We suggest an aspirin for your many troubles;
What remains of the night is ours to dissolve.

What stronger perfume than a just cause?
We hunger for change, and, where nothing moves, the milk in the
        dish coagulates;
A sleeping dog whimpers for the missing bone.
Such times these are, men who would aim true foul the line,
Say honour is not what is, but what we prescribe.

4

You made crazy promises for crazy times.
A wily magician, could he have conjured hope, would have ridden
Upon the shoulders of the populace.
A shabby god could be had at any price.
With the mood so ripe, you never slipped once.
So when did you begin to notice a drop in the temperature?
When the mammas stopped sending cakes?
The festive air of May shook with your fire.
The dead lay sprawled all over the place, their wounds bright
As the flags which the living brought here.
Later, you would put the slaughter down to a mistake,
As though a mistake could never be a crime.
Who, then, did you suppose the people were?
Despair had begun to gnaw at your vigilance,
And, as if on purpose, you would stray into the open spaces where
Any punk could draw a bead on fame.
You were destroyed as you deserved to be, by love.
Yes, you who would not allow the heart to meddle with your
        schemes
Put faith in a man who wore white shoes.
You lay as brothers side by side, the smoke of your cigarettes
Yellowing the white, while outside, the law would fake the
        circumstances
Of your demise, as though in this place
There can be no such thing as a straight line.
You slept beneath the Judas gaze, only to awake into death's embrace.
The news some hack had prepared well in advance sang through the
        wires.
The *signora,* your mother, sank to her knees;
With the cameras clicking around her in a circle,
She pressed her lips to where you'd bled over the cobble-stones,
        crying, *O sangue mio.*
You were already on the mortician's stone,
Bits of plaster from the death mask sticking to your face,
A player right down to the grand finale.

The *carabiniere* puzzled over your corpse,
Wondering how so much comes of so little.

Salvatore Giuliano, you may go as you please.
There is nobody here who'll divulge your crimes,
And besides, when the law frolics beneath the blanket with the
      knave
What's easier than to bribe a judge?
There has been a change in the climate, too,
Which will make recognition barely possible.
The features of all we know rapidly dissolve.
What can the gelding world say of brigandage,
When young women carry guns close to themselves, snugly as babes,
And when, instead of prayer, we place charms among the machines?
All things high and low slide towards the middle.
There is nothing solid we can put a face to.

5

We shed by slow degrees our disquietude.
The sun edges the hills with burning magnesium white,
And the hawk shadows the creeping snake.
All things wriggle into their familiar modes.
A stallholder handles with care the dark glow of aubergines.
A grocer scoops a pound of olives, so precise the reckoning of hand
      and eye.
We find in this a deeper resonance,
A play ghosting the whole of many lives.
Any worthy thing comes, shall come, of balance.
We called him who would become resolute in hate honourable,
And in doing so filled our house with shame.
The shutters open wide, we must go to our chores.
Our sullen desperadoes fade into the blankness of the page,
Sighing, *We shall be brought down by love.*

Shiraz

for Zahra Hashemi

I fell there into a strange kind of love.
A girl crushing darkness with a pestle,
She bled a thousand poisons from my eyes.
Said she, a winged creature filling her voice,
May Allah free you of all jealousies.

We sat weightless with joy at Hafiz' grave,
Spoke of many things that could never be
And of other things, too, full of substance.
We saw the moon climb above orange trees.
And we glowed, stupid with intelligence.

A woman, a dark mound of silence, came.
She fell to her knees, and pressing her face
Against the cool marble, raced her fingers
Through the flesh-coloured petals scattered there,
As though he, in death, had become flowers.

I asked my companion what tears these were
And for whom they spilled, Hafiz or her love.
She shivered, turned her face away from me,
Said there was much she had no language for
And still more a heart full dare not set free.

Later, she took Hafiz down from her shelves,
And, opening at the place her fingers chose,
She chanced upon words that flew to the core:
A stranger to my town comes, welcome him.
And for his pains may he now find a cure.

Uzbek Variations

for Monâjât Yultchieva

A saffron flowers on the slope.
Will you ever speak my name?

All night, sleep fled my eyes.
I warmed only frozen space.

★

A calf on a hill makes a noise,
Says, I am a full-grown mare.

A bride weeps in the house,
Says, Allah, I am a stranger.

★

Go, paint the leg of your horse
With henna my heart bleeds.

With the sinews of my life,
Sir, tie up your barking dog.

★

Quickly man destroys the house
Whose beams he put up with care.

She who prays he might change
Scrubs the raven's wing white.

★

Wash me with flowered water,
Sew me into a shroud of leaves.

May these tears the wind blows
Wet the blossom of your face.

Sparrows

Sparrows

The bitch muse has gone, pulled another fast one.
She knows better than you what makes things shake.
She has taken even the electric blanket and the ice cube maker,
The silver spoon in which she cooks her substances.
        She paints her fingernails blue.
A small space between her front teeth is so irresistible
She becomes second wife to a thousand men, none of whom
        realises he's not her only one.
You should have known better than to bring her home.
You should never have tried to work miracles on a global scale.
There are, after all, limits to what a man on stilts can do.

You bagged for yourself only history's brighter plumage.
It is time now to make amends, apologise for the massacre that took
        place
One cloudless afternoon, when Stone Age became Bronze Age,
When all talk was of modification to arrow structure and of wind
        velocity
And of how things would never again be quite the same.
Still, those old iniquities put your daily ones in the shade.
They are not without their uses. You are contrite, remember.
Squeeze just enough juice from your eyes, go on, twitch a little; the
        masses will swoon at your side.
Easy now, otherwise you will pay a heavy price for what you pretend
        not to be,
A surly lout who burps the ghost of an evening's beer.

        You ask, 'What's missing?'
Staring out the window, you rack your brain for a name to
A thing so obvious, one barely noticed while it was still there.
You do an exercise, skip over the alphabet for memory traces.
A sharper man than you would have kept some kind of score, might
        have seen wealth where you saw none.

Alzheimer's is in the culture, too.
Once, a friendly breeze would take you almost everywhere.
Once, the brandy was inhaled from brandy glasses;
	There was *bienséance*.
When all the particulars go, the world's skin will become a mass of
	sores.
It will not be, after all, cultivation that kills the jungle.

Who, then, will remember your bold squiggles,
All those endless glosses on a bottomless psyche?
She whom you took for a sort of wife tricked you into
Thinking there were at least a decade ahead of your time, hence the
	reluctance
Of the world's players to gamble on your rhymes.
An odalisque, a blush against emerald cushions, supine,
She looked as though she could soak up all of language.
Ha, did you really think your lines would keep her in one place?
She had ideas beyond anything you could imagine.

A mothballed ghost rises to your skull's centre.
Slowly you turn the pages of a book stippled with white spores.
What the words do is make you see crazy pictures:
A man cools his face against a pillar of rose marble;
Seven yellow wasps nuzzle a bowl of green grapes.
A Babylonian chorus cries, *If a man fails at what he loves,*
	God forbid he should succeed at what he hates.
The actors dropping their masks reveal themselves for what they
	always were,
Ordinary folk who could not resist the pull of the stage.
You never noticed them as you should have, in life.
Superannuated, they go off to their summer cottages,
Calm stations between what never was or will ever be.
She's gone, too, who wore rings in strange places, kohled her eyes,
And asked, in a husky voice, what your pleasure was.
All you could do, perfect fool, was bite your tongue.
Meanwhile, the sun's a broken yolk at the city's edge.

One by one the lights flicker on and the couple opposite gesticulate
        with their pizza slices
As if in some dumb ballet that you yourself choreograph as you
        watch
And puzzle at what goes on between other creatures.
You wonder, too, where have all the sparrows gone?

Notes

THE WATER CLOCK: 'When in AD 807 the great Haroun al Rashid sent an embassy to Charlemagne, among the presents brought to the western emperor was "a clock made with wonderful mechanical skill (*arte mechanica mirifice compositum*) driven by water and showing the twelve hours which are sounded by an appropriate number of small bronze bells dropping into a brass basin. At noon twelve horsemen come out of twelve windows which close behind them." Eginhard *(Annales,* ad annum) to whom we are grateful for this information added that "there are many other things in this clock", and his words disclose the astonishment and the admiration that the Arabian clock aroused at the Frankish court.' – Carlo M. Cipolla: *Clocks and Culture* (London, 1967), p. 25.

DEAD LOVERS: Dante's *Inferno:* Canto V, ll. 50–51.

COAST: 'Does he not say he will not strike his spars to any gale? Has he not dashed his heavenly quadrant? and in these same perilous seas, gropes he not his way by mere dead reckoning of the error-abounding log?' – Melville: *Moby Dick*, Chapter CXXIII.

THE WOLF MONTH: I am indebted to J. E. Harting's *British Animals Extinct Within Historical Times* (London, 1880).

TIGER MUSIC: The poem owes much, including several phrases, to a chapter in Marmaduke Pickthall's *Oriental Encounters* (1904). I was informed by my friend Subhi in Damascus that in Arabic there are sixty-seven words for 'lion'; I assume, perhaps wrongly, that there must be almost as many for 'tiger'.

A SEVENTH JEW: This poem has its origins in an incident that came to light during the Klaus Barbie trial. Seven members of the French Resistance in Lyon were arrested, imprisoned, and shortly afterwards executed; we know the identities of six of the people but of the seventh only that he was Jewish and that before being taken from his cell to be shot he sang Mario Cavara-dossi's aria from Act III of Puccini's *Tosca*. The opening lines of the poem draw from an uncredited translation of the libretto.

DINU LIPATTI PLAYS CHOPIN'S SONATA IN B MINOR: The Romanian pianist, Dinu Lipatti (1917–1950), was famously described by Walter Legge as having 'the shoulders of a wrestler'. The few recordings he made are, in almost every instance, considered by many to be 'definitive' readings of the works he chose. These performances are all the more remarkable because Lipatti was already suffering terribly from the cancer that would soon take his life. There are a couple of lines in the poem that draw from Walter Legge's article on Lipatti in the February 1951 issue of *Gramophone* maga-zine. Certain of the musical ideas and a phrase or two owe their existence to Victor Zuckerkandl's *Sound and Symbol, Music and the External World* (Rout-ledge & Kegan Paul, 1956).

THE CHARTERHOUSE AT VALLDEMOSA: George Sand, born Aurore Dupin, and the consumptive Frédéric Chopin went to Majorca in the autumn of 1838 hoping to find there an improving climate, and over three months experienced what was to be one of the island's coldest winters in decades. That Chopin survived at all was due to George Sand's diligence and common sense. Ill though he was, Chopin managed to complete his remarkable *24 Preludes*, op. 28. The odd circumstances behind the composition of the so-called 'Raindrop Prelude', no. 15, in D flat major, are recounted in Sand's memoirs, *Histoire de ma vie* (1848), and it is from this work and her account of their stay at the almost deserted Carthusian monastery at Valldemosa, *Un Hiver à Majorque* (1840), that I have drawn several apt phrases. The closing lines of the poem are from a letter written by Sand, on February 26th, 1839, to Charlotte Marliani.

COMMUNIQUÉ FOR WILLIAM HOFFER: William Hoffer (1944–1997). 'There are many of us who looked upon Bill Hoffer as a cross between a subversive philosopher, an unfulfilled bookseller and some kind of genius,' wrote Paul Minet in an obituary of him. Certainly, he was one of the best poets not to have written verse. Exasperated with the Canadian literary scene, whose fiercest critic he was, he closed his bookshop in Vancouver and moved to Moscow. A man with his hair combed back, he said, always looks as if he is going somewhere. After announcing, late one night, on a crackling telephone line, his abandonment of the English language he married a Russian, Masha Averyanova, with whom he collected some four thousand wooden toys. The poem is a collaboration with its subject who, really, has no choice in the matter. I have pulled a number of lines from his letters to me and from another, a small masterpiece of invective, which he wrote to a poet whose several volumes he particularly disliked. The military terminology is in no small measure a nod towards Hoffer's own use of the same, particularly in his rôle of Commander in Chief of TANKS, not so much a publishing venture as a one-man *zeitgeist*. I have never grown orchids.

AURORA BOREALIS: The italicized passages are from George Johnston's poem 'Poor Edward' first published in his collection *The Cruising Auk* (Oxford University Press, Toronto, 1959).

SALVATORE GIULIANO: 'Sicily is a metaphor for the modern world' – Leonardo Sciascia. Salvatore 'Turridu' Giuliano (1922–1950) was arguably the last Sicilian bandit worthy of note, although any greatness we might attribute to him is diminished by the folly of some of his ambitions. Among the most impractical of these was that Sicily be made the 49th American state, a proposal to which President Truman did not rise. With over a hundred slayings attached to his name, Giuliano may have had some hankering for a cause. I have composed nothing of biographical value here. A somewhat glamorized, though properly inclusive, account of his life may be found in Gavin Maxwell's *God Protect Me From My Friends* (Longman, Green and Co., London, 1956), and a more rigorously investigated one in Billy Jaynes Chandler's *King of the Mountain* (Northern Illinois University Press, DeKalb, 1988). As must always be the case, no one book about a bandit and his ambiguities can satisfy whole. Among the problems hardest to resolve is Giuliano's part in the shooting down of men, women and children at an outdoor Communist rally, the infamous Portella della Ginestra incident, although, to give him his say, he claimed to have been unaware of what took place. In true bandit fashion, Giuliano was betrayed by his close friend, Gaspare Pisciotta, but mystery still surrounds the circumstances. There is no hard evidence that Gaspare ever wore white shoes, and, among other liberties the poem takes, the ghostly gang which stalks its pages bears no resemblance to any persons dead or alive. The sacrifice of the snake is an ancient, presumably pagan, Sicilian charm against crop failure.

UZBEK VARIATIONS: Several of the lines are adaptations from translations of Persian poetry, more specifically those heard in the songs of the Sufi singer, Monâjât Yultchieva, and printed in the booklet accompanying her recording *Ouzbekistan* (Ocora/ Radio France C 560060).